# Feath & Furry Friends at the Farm

by
Cherie Brooks Reilly
Ryan and Katie Kerr

*Illustrated by Carol Stavish*
*Cover Design by Sam Oberdick*

Trafford
PUBLISHING®

Order this book online at www.trafford.com
or email orders@trafford.com

Most Trafford titles are also available at major online book retailers.

Illustrated by Carol Stavish

Co-authored by Ryan and Katie Kerr
Cover Design/Artwork by Sam Oberdick

Printed in the United States of America.

ISBN: 978-1-4669-4095-6 (sc)
ISBN: 978-1-4669-4094-9 (e)

Trafford rev. 06/19/2012

 www.trafford.com

North America & international
toll-free: 1 888 232 4444 (USA & Canada)
phone: 250 383 6864 ♦ fax: 812 355 4082

# Dedication

**Mimi...**

This book is dedicated to Grandmothers everywhere who love, teach and nurture their grandchildren. I never imagined that Grandmotherhood would be so much fun!

**Ryan**...

This book is dedicated to Grandpa Reilly who works very hard on his farm because he loves it.

**Katie**...

This book is dedicated to the Reilly and Kerr families and to all the animals who live on the farm.

# Acknowledgements

We are very grateful to professor Carol Stavish for using her vacation time to create such delightful, whimsical drawings. Her illustrations bring our stories to life.

Christina Wiedmann and Sam Oberdick have our heartfelt gratitude for using their computer talents to organize this project.

# Contents

# About This Book

Nestled among the hills along the Ohio River in the Southwestern corner of Pennsylvania is Reilly's 'Summer Seat' Farm. The name originated from the Land Grant title because this farm was once part of the Depreciation Lands given to George Washington's troops for their service in the Revolutionary War.

When Lt. Col Michael Reilly retired from the Marine Corps in 1983, he bought the acreage from his father with the dream of making it into a working farm. Even though farming was on the decline, Mike, with the help of his wife Cherie, and their children Renee, Michael, Kevin and Shawn, managed to create a productive farm and later added a garden center.

Over the years, **Summer Seat Farm** became synonymous with FUN, because of it's pick-your-own crops and exciting Fall Festivals which featured hayrides, pumpkin-picking, and an abundance of exciting autumn activities.

As the Reilly children grew and pursued their own careers in other parts of the country, only daughter Renee remained in the Pittsburgh area. Her children spent many happy hours chasing butterflies, picking berries, and enjoying the freedom of the farm. They welcomed the baby animals that arrived, and found appropriate names for all of them.

The grandchildren, Ryan and Katie Kerr, brought new vitality to Summer Seat Farm. When Ryan suggested that they write stories about the humorous and exciting events that happened at the farm, their grandmother (Mimi) agreed that it would be a wonderful way to preserve those special memories. Ryan (age 13), and Katie (age 11) wrote about some of their favorite animals and used the computer to research facts about other farm friends.Mimi added some remembrances of her own and organized it into a book.

Eight of the stories happened on Reilly's Summer Seat Farm. *The Goose Twins* occurred on the farm in South Dakota where Mimi grew up. The Last Story, <u>*Suzy Strawberry*</u>, is a fanciful tale about an imaginary strawberry plant that is used to teach children about strawberries and kindness. Mimi tells this story to school children who come to visit the farm.

Ryan, Katie and Mimi hope that you enjoy this book and that it will remind you of the many happy adventures that you once had on your own grandfather's farm.

Chapter One

# THE DAY WE TAUGHT THE DUCKS TO SWIM

## By Cherie Brooks Reilly
## With Ryan & Katie Kerr

*There's a little white duck sitting on the water,*
*a little white duck doing what he oughter.*
*He took a bite of a lily pad,*
*flapped his wings and he said,*
*"I'm glad I'm a little white duck sitting on the*
*water. Quack! Quack! Quack!"*

*Children's song by Walt Whippo*

Cherie Brooks Reilly • Ryan and Katie Kerr

# The Day We Taught The Ducks To Swim

By Cherie Brooks Reilly

Hi, my name is Ryan, and that's my sister, Katie. She's usually a pest, but sometimes we have fun together – like the day we taught the ducks to swim.

I'll tell you about it.

We have a grandmother who lives on a farm. We call her Mimi because 'Grandma' sounds so old.

In the springtime Mimi ordered some baby ducks from the hatchery.

The ducklings came in the mail and the postman smiled when he handed us the quacking box.

We helped our grandmother make a nice nest of straw for the fluffy yellow babies in a pen in the barn.

Mimi put a heat lamp above the pen because the ducklings didn't have a mother to keep them warm.

I put a dish of ground-up corn in the pen, and Katie put in a bowl of water. The little ducks soon stopped quacking and settled down for a nap.

It was fun to watch the baby ducks grow bigger and bigger.

One day when the baby ducks were about two weeks old, Katie said, "The poor ducklings have no mother. Who will teach them how to swim?"

We felt very sad for them.
Then I had a good idea.
"**We** can teach the ducks to swim!" I said.

We ran to get Mimi. She helped us put the ducklings in a box. Katie and I carried the box down to the pond.

Carefully I lifted one baby duck out of the box and set him on the water.

The fluffy duck floated, but he was afraid. He paddled his feet as fast as he could. He went around and around in a circle. He tried to climb out of the pond, but the sides were too high.

Then the duckling stopped paddling and just sat quietly on the water for a minute.

The duckling decided that he liked the water! He began to happily paddle around in the pond, splash, and dive under the water.

One by one Katie and I gently set all of the ducklings on the pond.

The ducklings swam and they splashed. They dove under the water and popped up. They chased each other and had races. They had a wonderful pool party!

We were sorry when it was time to take them back to their pen in the barn.

Mimi told us that, on the inside, the ducklings always knew how to swim. She called it an instinct. Katie and I gave the baby ducks a chance to do something that came naturally for them.

Mimi said that people have instincts, too. I wonder what mine are?

## Duck Facts and Tracks

**Female:** Duck    **Male:** Drake
(Commonly both are called ducks)
**Babies:** Ducklings    **Group:** Flock
**Incubation period:** Eggs hatch in 23 to 30 days, depending on the species.
**Number of eggs:** usually 5 to 12
**Favorite foods:** water plants and animals, insects, seeds, fruit and bugs.
**Life Span:** 2 to 12 years, depending on the species.

## Interesting facts about ducks:

1.  All ducks were once wild until the Chinese domesticated them hundreds of years ago.

2.  Ducks are related to swans and geese.

3.  Wild ducks migrate to warmer places in the winter.

4.  Ducks are found in all parts of the world except

Antarctica.

5.  Baby ducks have an egg tooth on their bill when they are inside the shell. This sharp tooth helps them open the shell so they can get out. It disappears a few days after they hatch.

6.  Most ducklings can run, swim, and find food by themselves on the day they hatch.

7.  Most ducklings look alike and a new mother accepts all of them. If a new mother quacks loudly and swims around with her duckling where there are other families of ducks, she may attract other youngsters and end up with 20 to 40 ducklings while other females end up with only 2 or 3.

8.  Ducks have webbed feet, which act like paddles, so they prefer swimming to walking and have an awkward waddle on land.

9.  Duck's feet have no nerves or blood vessels so they don't feel the cold even when they swim in icy water.

10. The feathers on ducks are waterproof. Ducks have a special gland near their tail that produces

oil. This oil spreads over their outer feathers and makes them waterproof. Under that layer, ducks has fluffy, Soft feathers, called down, that keep them warm.

Chapter Two

# HELLO, MR. COW

## by Ryan Kerr

*The friendly cow all red and white*
*I love with all my heart:*
*She gives me cream with all her might,*
*To eat with apple-tart.*

*The Cow by Robert Louis Stevenson*

# Hello Mr. Cow

## by Ryan Kerr

It was toward the end of a regular day at Evans City Middle School when suddenly a voice came over the loudspeaker in the fifth grade classroom, "Would Ryan Kerr please come to the office."

Any other day I would have been worried that I was in trouble, but this day was special. I proudly walked to the office because I knew that it was my Grandfather who was picking me up. We were going to the Amish animal auction. We needed new baby animals for the school tours coming up soon at Summer Seat Farm, and he wanted a kid's opinion on what animals to buy.

When I got to the office Grandpa was standing there just as excited as I was.

The principal asked, "Do you know this man?"

"Yes, he's my grandfather," I answered.

"Okay, you can go," He replied and we rushed out the door.

Grandpa and I were both excited to get the new animals, and spend some quality time together. We drove to my sister Katie's school and picked her up so she could help choose the animals too. In a few minutes we were buckled up in Grandpa's van and ready for the long journey to New Wilmington, Pennsylvania.

After a long and boring ride, we jumped out of the van and saw many Amish men dressed in straw hats and black clothes gathering at the auction barn. Their horses and buggies were in the shade under the trees close by. Katie and I looked at each other with even more excitement because we both knew the Amish were some of the best farmers around, so we knew the animals were going be good and healthy. We stepped into the big auction barn and saw many people crowding around fences with animals inside. Grandpa, Katie, and I pushed our way through the crowd to get to the little fence filled with all types of calves. There were tall ones, small ones, fat ones, skinny ones, and colorful ones. Katie and I looked over the fence and grinned at the sight of all those calves.

"Hello, Mr. Cow," I said to the calf closest to me that was looking up with big brown eyes.

"It's either Mrs. Cow or Mr. Bull", Grandpa said.

"You can't have it both ways. Most of these are boy calves because many of the Amish people are dairy farmers and they keep their girl calves to produce milk later on."

We picked our favorites calves and named them. Grandpa told us to stick out our hand and see which calves would suck on it because that would let us know which calves were hungry and were ready to be bottle-fed. Katie and I put our hands into the pen and then we both squealed, because now there was slobber all over our hands!

It was time for the auction to begin so Grandpa, Katie and I hurried to find our seats.

"The auction for calves will now begin," said the auctioneer.

The first few calves came out one by one and were put up for bid. The men brought in one of the calves that Katie and I liked, and we poked grandpa and pointed to the brown calf.

"Do I hear 10 cents a pound?" the announcer asked. Grandpa raised his bidding card quickly.

"11 cents a pound."

An Amish guy behind us raised his card.

The auctioneer was talking very fast and the bidding kept going up and up until Grandpa decided it was too high and he stopped bidding.

We were disappointed at first, but then another calf that Katie and I liked came up for bid. Grandpa raised his card, but the same thing happened. Somebody kept bidding higher. We began to worry that we wouldn't get a calf that we liked. Finally the last calf we had picked came up for bid, and we hoped that Grandpa could afford it.

Grandpa bid 15 cents, but the Amish man behind us bid 16. The auctioneer kept talking and Grandpa raised his card again. We waited for someone to bid higher, but nobody did! We finally had a calf. Katie jumped up and down with excitement. I couldn't stop smiling as we went down to pick up our calf. When we saw it up close again, we were very surprised that no one else bid on it, because it was such a pretty little black and white calf. I helped Grandpa load our new animal into the van.

"Why didn't anyone else bid on our calf," I asked Grandpa on the way home.

Grandpa thought for a minute and then said, " I'm

not sure, but I think the Amish men saw that you really wanted that calf and they stopped bidding. The Amish are very family oriented, you know. I think I'm really lucky that you came with me."

## Cow Facts and Tracks

**Other names:** Cattle

People commonly use the term 'cow' for both male and female cattle.

**Male:** Bull    **Female:** Cow

**Baby:** Calf    **Group:** herd

A young cow is called a heifer.

**Gestation period:** 9 months

**Favorite food:** grass, grain and silage, which is made from fermented corn and hay.

**Life span:** up to 25 years

### Interesting facts about cattle:

1.  People have raised cattle for thousands of years and on every continent except Antarctica.

2.  There are many breeds of cattle that are classified according to their purpose. Beef cattle are raised for meat and leather, and dairy cattle are raised to give milk.

3.  Cattle have four compartments in their stomach. They quickly swallow food and then bring it back up from their stomach and chew and digest it when they are resting. This regurgitated food is called a cud.

4.  Cows have long tails which they use to shoo away insects.

5.  Cattle are hearty eaters. A two-year old cow can consume 25 pounds of silage, 4 pounds of hay, and 15 pounds of corn in a day.

6.  India has more cattle than any other country, but they are considered sacred animals and cannot be eaten.

7.  Cattle are mostly color-blind so they do not see the red cape of a Bull Fighter; instead the bull is attracted by the movement of the cape.

8.  Cattle are less intelligent than most domesticated animals.

9.  A cow has a baggy organ called an udder that hangs from the cow's body a little in front of its back legs. It has four sections that hold the milk.

10. Cattle cannot bite grass off because they do not

have cutting teeth. Instead, they tear off the grass by moving their head.

Chapter Three

# MIRACLES

## by Katie Kerr

*On a bluff, on a bluff,*
*There lived three Billy goats Gruff*
*Little Billy Goat, Bigger Billy Goat,*
*Great Big Billy Goat Gruff.*

*Children's song: Three Billy Goats Gruff*

# Miracles

by Katie Kerr

Some people don't believe in miracles, but on Summer Seat Farm, miracles happen every day. All of the animals that live on the farm have their own story and are the result of their own special miracle.

The first miracle that I'll tell you about happened on the day before Christmas. Grandpa usually sets up a manger scene at the Garden Center because Baby Jesus was born in a manger. He brings several animals from the barn and puts them in a pen by the manger so people can get the feeling of how things were on that first Christmas. Last year he put a calf, a lamb and a goat in the pen. I thought Big Mama Goat looked like she was going to burst, but no one else seemed to notice. On the day before Christmas when I was visiting the farm, I decided to go down to the Garden Center to look at the Christmas trees. When I passed the animal pen, I saw two tiny little goats standing in the corner by big Mama! Grandpa said they were born during the night. Since one was a boy and the other a girl and they were born the day before Christmas, my brother and I named them

Mary and Joseph.

Another miracle happened about two years ago. It was the week before Christmas and every body was very busy getting ready, but the work for one mother sheep was done. When we came to the farm for Christmas dinner, my Grandmother, Mimi, said there was a surprise up in the barn. My brother Ryan and I went up to look, and we saw the mother sheep lying on the hay with twin lambs. We were surprised because most of the animals are born in the spring when it's warmer. Goats are strong so they don't mind the cold, but little lambs are more delicate. The lambs were so tiny and one could barely stand up. We tried to decide on some names for them, but we couldn't agree. When we came back the next day, we found only one lamb. Grandpa said that the other one wasn't strong enough to survive, and it had died during the night. We decided to name the strong lamb *One-of-a-Kind*.

The last miracle that I'll tell you about is one that frightened me at first. Mimi and I went up to the barn to feed the animals. Mimi went up to the top of the barn to get some hay. I stepped into the bottom of the barn, but suddenly I saw something black moving. It almost looked like a shadow. I was scared because I knew they found a rat in the barn last summer. I decided to wait until Mimi came back. When Mimi returned, I followed her into the barn. After our eyes got used to the dark, we saw ten baby chicks running about in all directions following their mother as she scratched for food. All of them were black with a big white dot on top of their head. They looked like they had been made by a copy machine. That was the first time a chicken had hatched out that many eggs. We tried to name them, but we couldn't tell them apart so we just gave them numbers and it didn't matter which number they got.

Some people say these were just surprise births, but I think that any time something is born it is a little miracle. Don't you?

## Goat Facts and Tracks

<u>**Male:**</u> Buck or Billy    <u>**Female:**</u> Nanny or Doe
<u>**Babies**</u>: Kids   <u>**Group:**</u> herd
<u>**Gestation period**</u>: 146 to 155 days
<u>**Favorite food**</u>: Grass, weeds, shrubs, and almost any vegetation.
<u>**Life span**</u>: 10 to 14 years

### <u>Interesting facts about goats:</u>

1. Goats are sometimes called the "poor man's cow" because they don't need as much care as a cow, and they provide meat and milk.

2. Goats have a special stomach so they can swallow food quickly and later chew it as a **cud**, much like a cow.

3. Goats are raised throughout the world and their milk is white, sweet, nourishing, and easier to digest than cow's milk.

4. Beautiful clothing and rugs are made from the hair of goats. Cashmere and Angora goats are two breeds that have hair that is made into fine clothing.

5. A nanny goat usually gives birth to one, two or three kids.

6. Most goats have beards, even the females.

7. Baby goats are born fully haired with their eyes open. They can run and jump four hours after birth.

8. The pupil of a goat's eye is rectangular instead of round. They have excellent night vision.

9. Female goats weigh between 22 and 220 pounds, and male goats weigh between 27 and 275 pounds, depending on the breed.

10. The age of a goat can be closely determined by its teeth.

# Chapter Four

# BEAUTY'S SECRETS

## As told by Jody Jackson and Sally Oberdick

*Ride a Cock-Horse to Banbury Cross*
*To see a fine lady upon a white horse;*
*Rings on her fingers and bells on her toes,*
*And she will have music wherever she goes.*

*Nursery Rhyme from Mother Goose*

# Beauty's Secrets

(Based on Information from Sally Oberdick and Jody Jackson of Pepper Hill Farm)

"She can really run fast," declared 8-year old Tommy.

The boys and girls attending Sally Oberdick's Farm Camp walked across the field toward Pepper Hill Farm to visit Beauty, the chestnut-colored horse that lived next to Summer Seat Farm. When the mare heard them coming, she picked up her ears and galloped toward the fence. She knew that children's voices meant special treats. Beauty stopped abruptly at the split rail fence and accepted the morsels that were held high by tiny fingers.

"She sure is big," said Kevin. "I bet she could beat any horse in a race."

Everyone agreed that Beauty was the fastest and best horse in the whole world.

If Beauty could talk, she would have told the children some amazing secrets about her life. She had been bred to be a racehorse. Her father was a champion and had won many races. Her owner hoped that Beauty would follow in his hoof prints.

The colt was a wonderful sight to behold as she flew across the green pasture, neck arched, tail straight out, taking long strides. Her former owner even had her lip tattooed by the Thoroughbred Race Association. She was given the official name of "Red Zoomer".

Unfortunately, however, as Beauty grew in size, she didn't grow in speed. After a few races, her owner discovered that she wasn't a zoomer. She was just a prancer. He put her up for sale in a claimer's race (a race where people can buy the losing horses). Her new owner took the filly to live in a hunter's stable. Now she was just part of the herd. Anyone could rent her.

Poor Beauty, she was no longer special. Would she ever find someone who would love and appreciate her, even though she was slow?

One cold day in January, a lady from Pepper Hill Farm came to the stable. She wanted to buy a horse for her daughter, Jody, who loved to go fox hunting and trail riding. The lady, Mrs. James, saw the sweet, gentle, reddish-brown mare and stopped to pat her on the nose. The horse nuzzled the lady's neck and Mrs. James fell in love immediately. She bought the young horse and renamed her *So Beautiful,* or <u>Beauty</u>

for short.

Mrs. James brought Beauty to live at Pepper Hill Farm. Her daughter Jody enjoyed watching the spirited horse run across the pasture, head held high, looking very regal. A horse named Toss-A-Bit already lived in the small gray barn at the farm and the two horses became good friends. They would stand head to rump and switch flies off each other with their long tails.

For many years Beauty and Toss-A-Bit shared the same barn and pasture. They went on exciting foxhunts and quiet walks through the woods together. Jody gave riding lessons and Beauty patiently took the children and adults on long rides while they practiced their horsemanship skills.

Toss-A-Bit was several years older, and Beauty was very sad and lonely when her stall-mate died. However, she soon found some new friends. They didn't live with Beauty, but after Toss-A-Bit died, they began to come for visits. The animals at Summer Seat Farm enjoyed venturing out of their own pasture and wiggled under the fence to spend some time with the pretty mare. Farmer Reilly's cow, sheep and goats stopped by for a few blades of grass. Reilly's helpers, Michele and Eric, eventually came and retrieved the wayward animals and led them back home. Beauty would stand at the fence and stare after them as if to say, "Thanks for stopping by, guys, I was lonely today."

Occasionally deer would wander into Beauty's pasture for a brief hello. They would never stay long and would move on with a graceful leap over the fence to munch on the tender twigs in the shady woods across the road.

Sometimes a stray dog would invade her field. The intruder would bark and try to scare her, but Beauty would just turn in his direction and toss her head in defiance and disgust. Her actions seemed to say, 'Why are you making such a fuss? I'm much bigger than you, and I don't think you're so tough'.

Her strangest friend and the one that became her best buddy, was Jasmine, the short-legged, very fat, pot-bellied pig. They would greet each other with a nose touch, and then Jasmine would put her front feet on Beauty's hocks and lick off all the mud and salt. It must have felt like a grand massage. The pretty chestnut mare stood very still and never kicked her portly pal.

However, of all the friends who came to visit, it was the children who gave Beauty the most pleasure. They brought her treats of grass, weeds, flowers, apples, and carrots. They patted her long neck and big nose with their little hands. Amid the oohs and aahs, they would proclaim, 'You are so beautiful', 'Can I ride you someday?' and 'Someday I want a horse just like you'.

Beauty accepted all the loving pats, adoration and tasty tidbits with great dignity and stood tall, nodding her head in appreciation.

## Horse Facts and Tracks

**Male**: Stallion or Sire (father of foal)

**Female**: Mare (over 4 years old)

**Names for young horses**: (1) Foal (newly born), (2) Colt (under 4 years old), (3) Filly (female under 4 years old), (4) Yearling (over 1 year old, but less than 2).

**Gestation period**: about 11 months (10 to 14, depending on breed)

**Favorite foods**: Grain (especially oats), hay (especially timothy, alfalfa, and clover). A horse needs salt. A horse needs 10 to 12 gallons of clean, fresh water a day.

**Life span: 20 to 30 years**

**Interesting facts about horses:**

1.    Horses were the most important means of travel

for thousands of years before cars were invented. Now horses are used mainly for recreational riding and racing.

2.  Small horses that are less than 58 inches tall are called <u>ponies</u>.

3.  Wild horses on the western plains of the U.S. are called <u>mustangs</u>. They are descendants of the horses that Spanish explorers brought to America. Indians tamed mustangs to help hunt buffalo. Later, cowboys rode them to herd cattle.

4.  A horse needs to eat three times a day because it has a small stomach.

5.  Most horses have good memories and can be trained to obey commands. They are usually eager to please their master. They also remember punishment and things that frightened them.

6.  Horses come in many colors, combination and shades of black, brown, white and red, with special spots and markings.

7.  *Gait* refers to the way a horse moves. Horses have three natural gaits: (1) walk (2) run, and (3) trot.

8.  The first thing that a rider learns to do is mount

(get on) the horse. Riders should mount from the left side. Mounting on the right side confuses the horse.

9. Horseshoes protect the horse's hoofs especially when they walk on hard surface. These are U-shaped pieces of iron that are nailed to the horse's hoofs.

10. An expert horseman can tell the age of the horse by counting its teeth. A foal is born toothless.

Chapter Five

# SURPRISE KITTENS

## by Ryan Kerr

*Pussy cat, Pussy cat,*
*Where have you been?*
*I've been to London to visit the queen.*
*Pussy cat, Pussy cat,*
*What did you there?*
*I frightened a little mouse under her chair.*

*Nursery Rhyme from Mother Goose*

# Surprise Kittens

by Ryan Andrew Kerr

A few years ago Lily the cat was having her first batch of kittens at Reilly's Summer Seat Farm. Slowly but surely, one by one, they all came out of Lily's womb. The first kitten was the largest, and that kitten drank the fastest. It was also the prettiest. It was a darker shade of black with a hint of white. It took a while before Lily had another kitten but we waited patiently because some things just can't be rushed. The healthy second kitten was fairly large, and was a beautiful shade of grayish white. Lily lay quietly, licking her first born and gathering her strength.

I was starting to think that Lily was only going to have two kittens, and I had just gotten up off my knees and was about to go inside the house, when she began to give birth to the third kitten. It was rather small, but still healthy, and it was the same shade of gray as the second kitten. The fourth kitten followed quickly behind the third kitten, and was also a dark shade of gray.

After taking so long to give birth, the new mother lay nursing her young for a while. We were surprised when her got up and headed up the hill to the barn. We thought she would be exhausted.

When my grandpa came up to the house, he saw the kittens lying under the bench on the deck, crying.

"Where is the mother cat?" he asked. "These kittens need to be in a warm place, and they're probably hungry, too."

"She went up to the barn. She's probably hungry and went to look for mice. This is all new to her," I reminded him, so he wouldn't think badly of Lily.

Grandpa Reilly put the kittens in the warm doghouse on a nice soft blanket. When Lily came back to the house, grandpa showed her where he had placed her newly born family. Lily cuddled up inside the doghouse, and began to nurse her four little kittens. Suddenly she ran back up to the barn. Grandpa and I didn't know what was going on, but we thought that Lily was just going to hunt again.

After watching the kittens cry for a few minutes, Grandpa and I went into the house to eat our dinner. When we finished our dinner, my sister Katie wanted to see the new kittens, so we went to the side porch and peeked into the doghouse. Katie looked at the kittens in amazement, and started to name them one by one. She named the four kittens Oddball, Mo, Dumbo, and Charles. While Katie still watched the babies wiggle around inside of the doghouse, I went into the house to watch TV.

Shortly after I went inside, Katie began to scream loudly, "Ryan! Grandpa! Come quick!"

Grandpa and I ran out of the house to see what had happened. Once we got to the side deck I asked, "What's wrong, Katie?"

Katie said, "Look inside the dog house."

Grandpa and I bent over and peeked into the doghouse. Lily lay in the back corner and she was nursing <u>six</u> beautiful kittens.

Katie said, "Lily brought two more kittens down from the barn in her mouth."

Grandpa and I were surprised.

"That's why Lily kept going up to the barn," I said, "I thought it was a little strange."

Katie said, "Let's name the two other kittens Courtney and Angel."

I agreed, and the kittens seemed to enjoy their

new names.

After the big commotion was over, Mom and my grandmother came outside to look at the new kittens that Lily had brought down from the barn. Mimi commented on how adorable the new kittens were. Mom didn't say much because she was afraid we'd ask to keep one. She did say that she was happy to see the little family because Katie and I would have new friends to play with when we came to visit the farm.

Three of the six beautiful kittens survived their first two months of life – Dumbo, Mo, and Angel. Lily mistakenly laid on the other three. After three months of living on the farm, Dumbo and Mo were adopted into good homes. Angel lived on the farm for about two years, and had a batch of kittens of her own. After living on the farm for two years she ran away, and was never found again. Katie and I believe that Angel is still alive, but she has another home somewhere in the woods.

On the other hand, Lily had three more batches of kittens while living on the farm. After about three years, we gave Lily to the Human Society because it was getting hard to adopt out the kittens and we were running out of mice. Lily now has a new loving owner who takes very good care of her.

This story is told by Ryan Kerr, and is based on a true happening. It is dedicated to Brandon, my favorite goat that recently passed away.

## Cat Facts and Tracks

**Other name**: **Feline**

**Cat** refers to both male and female

**Male**: Tom    **Babies:** Kittens

**Group of babies:** Litter

**Gestation period:** 2 months, so it's important to have cats spayed or the cat population will get out of control.

**Size:** Female cats usually weigh from 6 to 10 pounds, but tomcats may weigh from 9 to 17 pounds and some have reached over 30 pounds.

**Life Span:** 14 to 20 years, but some have lived past 30 years of age.

**Favorite food:** Dry or canned cat food. Make sure it's not red. Cats will eat vegetables and need clean fresh water.

## Interesting facts about cats:

1. Cats have many "wild" relatives (lions, tigers), but tame cats have provided faithful, friendly companionship to humans for thousands of years. Cats were even worshipped in ancient Egypt.

2. Cats are quite independent. They purr when they are happy and hiss when they are frightened or angry.

3. Cats sleep from 16-18 hours a day –longer than most other animals.

4. Some cats can run up to 30 miles an hour and can jump 7 times the length of their tail.

5. All cats are born with blue eyes. Kitten's eyes are sensitive to light so the mother cat usually finds a dark place to give birth and the kitten's eyes are closed for over two weeks.

6. Cats aren't colorblind; they can see green, blue, and red.

7. Cats have a good sense of smell – about 14 times greater than humans.

8. In the animal kingdom, a cat's I.Q. is surpassed

only by a monkey's and chimp's I.Q.

9.  Because of genetics, calico cats are always females.

10. A cat has 30 muscles in its ears and can rotate them 180 degrees. This allows a cat to hear in all directions without moving his head.

11. Stroking a cat can lower one's blood pressure.

# Chapter Six

# CHOCOLATE

## By Katie Kerr

*When brother takes me walking I cry, "Oh hip, hooray!*
*We're sure to see the jolly pup that joins us every day!"*
*His ears are raggy-shaggy: his coat's a dusty brown;*
*He meets me like a cannon ball and nearly*
*knocks me down*

*The Ordinary Dog by Nancy Byrd Turner*

# Chocolate

## by Katie Kerr

One day in June, my brother Ryan and I were attending Farm Camp at my Grandpa's farm. The teacher, Mrs. Oberdick, said, "We're going to go to the log cabin on top of the hill so I can show you something special."

"What do you think it is?" I asked Ryan as we walked up the hill.

"I don't know," he said, "But that is where the Beck family lives and I know they have lots of animals."

When we got to the log cabin, the teacher took us up on the porch. Curled up on a blanket was a long Bassett Hound with ten brand new puppies. They were so cute!

"They don't look like the mother," I said, looking at the puppies that were brown, and beige and lots of colors in between, and none of them had floppy ears.

"The father was a Labrador retriever that lives in the neighborhood," said Mrs. Beck, "and all the puppies are up for adoption except the beige one that my children want to keep."

Ryan and I played with all the puppies. We went

from one to the other because we couldn't decide which one we liked the best. The little black puppy kept following us, but we decided we liked the yellow one better. We planned how we were going to ask our mother if we could have one.

Ryan and I were with Mimi (our Grandmother) and Grandpa when Mom came to pick us up from camp. We told her about the adorable puppies and begged her to let us have one.

"Absolutely not." she said, "We don't have enough room in our townhouse for a dog."

Then I said, " Grandpa, you have lots of room, can we get a puppy and keep him here?"

Grandpa said, "We already have a dog." and walked down to the greenhouse.

"Please, Mimi, please," I begged with my most serious puppy-dog face.

"I'll talk to him," she said," but I don't think he'll give in."

We went home and felt sad.

The next day when we arrived at the farm for camp, Mimi greeted us with a little black puppy in her arms.

"Grandpa decided that you could have a puppy, but the yellow one was gone when I called the Becks." She said, "This was the only puppy left. Do you like this one?"

"Oh yes!" we said together.

We played with him all day and decided to call him Chocolate because he looked like rich dark chocolate. His whole name was Chocolate Hershey Reilly. Grandpa told us it was a girl, but we liked the name so we kept it anyway.

Every day Chocolate's body grew bigger and bigger, but her legs never did. She was so friendly that the children all loved her. Because she was quite long and low to the ground, several children could pet her at the same time. Chocolate thought it was her job to make everybody happy, and she brought a smile to every kid's face as she stood there getting petted and wagging her long tail. She loved to ride on the hay wagon with all the boys and girls who came to visit the farm, and she would jump right up on the wagon whenever the tractor started. Then she'd lie down on the hay and wait to get petted.

One day when Ryan, our friend Abby, and I were

playing with Chocolate, we decided to take her down the long plastic slide that my grandparents had made on the hillside. We pushed her down and she rolled over and over and tried to get up on her stubby little legs. We slid down behind her and we ended up in a pile at the bottom of the hill. We all laughed and ran up the hill to do it again.

Chocolate loved to play. One day we put her on the trampoline, but after we jumped a couple times, she decided to jump off. Wherever there were children, that's where we'd find Chocolate.

One day when Chocolate was playing on the hill behind the barn, my grandfather heard a gunshot and a yelp. He wondered what it was. A few minutes later, the people who gave us Chocolate, brought her down the hill. She had been shot! Grandpa rushed her to the vet, but it was too late. A bullet had hit her leg and had gone into her lung. The vet had to put her to sleep so she wouldn't suffer.

Mom brought us to the farm just as Grandpa was returning from the vet. Chocolate was in a little cardboard coffin that the vet had given to her. Grandpa sadly told us the tragic news and we cried and cried.

Grandpa asked if we wanted to see Chocolate and we said yes. We peeked inside the little box. She looked so peaceful. We wrote, "I love you" all over her coffin. Then we picked flowers and laid them on the box and said goodbye. Grandpa buried her next to the blueberry bushes on the hillside overlooking the farmhouse. We miss her very much.

R.I.P. Chocolate.

## Dog Facts and Tracks

**Other name:** Canine

**Dog** refers to all canines, regardless of age or sex

**Babies:** Puppies

**Group of adult dogs: Pack**

**Gestation period:** 58 to 63 days

**Purebred:** Parents are of the same breed

**Crossbreed:** Parents are two known breeds

**Mixed breed:** Parents are of mixed and unknown breeds.

**Favorite foods:** dog food may be dry or canned. It should be 1/3 meat. Drinking water should be available. Check with veterinarian to see if your dog needs vitamins or minerals.

## Interesting facts about dogs:

1.   Dogs were the first animals to be domesticated and have helped people in work, play and sports for over 10,000 years.

2.  A group of puppies born to one mother is called a litter. The mother usually has from 1 to 12 puppies but there have been litters of over 20 babies.

3.  Dogs mature in six months and usually live 8 to 15 years. The oldest dog on record was 29 years old.

4.  The smallest dog is a Chihuahua (5 in) The tallest is an Irish Wolf Hound (almost 3 ft.). The heaviest is a St. Bernard (180 lbs.)

5.  There are over 200 different breeds of dog. Mixed breeds are sometimes called mongrels and often make nice pets.

6.  Puppies are born blind, deaf and toothless and depend entirely on their mother for food and warmth for about four weeks.

7.  The fastest dog is the Whippet, which can run up to 35 miles an hour.

8.  A breed of dogs called Basenji is the only dog that does not bark.

9.  Dalmatian puppies are born all white and develop spots as they mature.

10. A dog can hear sounds 25 miles away. (People can hear about 25 yards)

11. Dogs can be taught to obey commands and are popular pets because most breeds are friendly and eager to please their master.

Chapter Seven

# THE CHRISTMAS GIFT

## by Cherie Brooks Reilly

*Little Bo-peep has lost her sheep,*
*And doesn't know where to find them;*
*Leave them alone and they'll come home,*
*Wagging their tails behind them.*

*Nursery Rhyme from Mother Goose*

# The Christmas Gift

by Cherie Brooks Reilly

Everybody at Summer Seat Farm was busily preparing for the holiday season. Freshly cut trees stood in neat rows so that people could easily find their special Christmas tree. Piles of wreaths, garland, and other seasonal greens lay on the long tables. In the greenhouse, Farmer Mike was decorating the pots of the poinsettias with festive red foil.

Foreman Michele used a bucket of food to coax a goat, a calf and a sheep with her lamb out of the turn-of-the-last-century barn. She led the animals to the market area where she placed them inside an improvised woven wire enclosure. Outside this pen was a manger where a Baby Jesus doll lay sleeping on the hay surrounded by statues of Mary, Joseph and the Wisemen. The children who came to visit this peaceful Nativity scene were fascinated by the live animals and reached their little hands over and through the fence to pet them. The animals seemed quite content to receive all this attention because they also received some kernels of corn with it.

Two weeks before Christmas, on a moonless

night, Farmer Reilly heard some barking and bleating sounds coming from the market area. The noise soon subsided so he turned over and went back to sleep. The next morning when he went to feed the animals, he saw that the lamb and the goat were missing. Something had frightened them during the night, perhaps a stray dog. They had bolted through a hole in the fence. Neither animal was in sight, for they had fled into the woods. The farmer knew it was impossible to find them in the densely wooded valleys.

Two days later a neighbor called.

"There's a lamb and goat grazing in my back yard," he said. "Are they yours?"

Farmer Reilly apologized and set out to retrieve his flock from the neighbor's yard. He brought some food and a rope. After scattering some food on the ground, Farmer Mike slipped the rope around the goat's neck when it came to eat. However, the frightened lamb plunged back into the woods again.

During the next few days, several neighbors called with lamb sightings. Someone saw the frightened little creature by the school, but it had disappeared by the time the farmer arrived. The neighbor at the top of the hill called, as well as someone about a mile away. However, when Farmer Reilly tried to approach the frightened little sheep, she always escaped into the trees and underbrush. The weather turned cold and storms were predicted. The lamb could not survive by herself in the wilderness, and the farmer was very concerned.

Two days before Christmas, the Ohio Township police car turned into the farm entrance.

When the patrolman reached the spot where the farmer was working, he stopped and said, "There's a little sheep at the edge of the woods just over the hill. If it belongs to you, I'll show you where it is."

Since Farmer Mike knew the timid lamb would not let any person approach her, he devised a new plan. He gathered up a bucket of grain with molasses – a favorite food of the animals. Placing a rope around the neck of the goat, he shook the pail of food - which was a signal for dinnertime at the barnyard. He began to lead the goat down the road. The mother sheep, not wanting to miss out on a meal, followed along just as the farmer had hoped. The policeman drove ahead to show the farmer where he had seen the lamb.

Upon reaching the area where the lamb was last sighted, the farmer scattered the grain on the ground and the goat and the ewe greedily began to eat. Suddenly the mother sheep lifted her head. A bedraggled little lamb appeared at the edge of the woods a good distance away. The mother recognized it and began to walk toward her baby. The frightened lamb looked as if she would flee, but the ewe continued to walk slowly toward her. The mother sheep put out her nose and touched the lamb's nose as if giving her a little kiss. The two animals stood there for several minutes happily nuzzling each other.

Then the ewe turned abruptly, motioned to her baby, and they walked back to the area where the goat was eating. The three animals quickly finished the grain. Farmer Reilly picked up the rope that hung from the goat's neck and tugged on it, signaling that it was time to go home. The goat obliged and let the farmer lead him back down the road. The sheep and her lamb followed along behind the goat. The policeman drove behind all of them with his lights flashing. The only thing missing from this strange procession was a brass band.

People pulled their cars over to the side of the road and smiled as the little Christmas parade passed by.

Upon reaching the farm, Farmer Mike led the animals to their pen. He opened the fence and the goat walked quietly inside, followed by the ewe and her baby. The farmer reached down and petted the lamb standing beside his mother.

"Welcome home, little fellow," he said.

After double-checking to be certain that the pen was securely fastened, Farmer Mike walked to his house. His mind was at peace because his animals were safe. The ewe and her lamb snuggled down on the hay close to each other. They seemed to know that they had received a wonderful Christmas gift.

## Sheep Facts and Tracks

**Male**: Ram  **Female:** Ewe

**Babies:** Lambs  **Group:** Flock

**Gestation period**: 5 months

**Favorite food:** grain and hay

**Life Span:** about 13 years

**Size**: Adults varies in weight from less than 100 pounds to over 350 pounds.

## Interesting facts about sheep:

1.  Originally wild sheep from Central Asia were tamed and raised for their hides and milk.

2.  Most sheep in the U.S. are raised for their wool, which is sheared off and made into warm clothing.

3.  Sheep are shorn once a year in the spring when it gets warm. The sheep shearer uses a special

clipper and can cut the wool or fleece off in a matter of minutes.

4. Sheep are raised in countries all over the world. China and Australia raise the most sheep.

5. Ewes usually give birth to one or two lambs, and sometimes three.

6. Sheep are raised in two ways: (1) on the open-range, where they roam freely and find their own food, and (2) confined in pens where food is brought to them.

7. A person who watches over the sheep is called a shepherd or sheep herder.

8. Spanish Merino sheep are prized for their fine wool and although there are several other breeds, Merino sheep are the most popular.

9. Lambs are born with long tails, but the tails are cut off so the wool stays cleaner.

10. Sheep are gentle and easily frightened. Sheep are very social animals and they like to stay together. If one sheep is separated from the flock, it may panic and become agitated.

Chapter Eight

# KILLER PIG

## by Cherie Brooks Reilly

*To market, to market, to buy a fat pig,*
*Home again, home again, jiggety-jig;*
*To market, to market, to buy a fat hog,*
*Home again, home again, jiggety-jog.*

*Nursery Rhyme from Mother Goose*

# Killer Pig

## by Cherie Brooks Reilly

"Kill the pig! Kill the pig!" screamed Katie, Ryan and Abby, as they scrambled up the pile of hay bales.

Startled by their frantic voices, Mimi, their grandmother, turned and looked at the pen behind them. The young pig in the pen had a chicken in his mouth and was shaking his head violently.

"Kill the pig! Kill the pig! He's eating the chicken!" screamed the children again, jumping up and down atop the bales.

"Stop that!" Mimi yelled at the pig, rushing to the pen.

The startled young pig dropped the limp chicken and turned his head toward her quizzically.

"Kill the pig, Mimi," pleaded Ryan. "He's dangerous!"

Not wanting the children to be afraid of the once-cute little pig, Mimi tried to soothe their cries.

"Now, now," she said calmly, "he's probably just hungry."

Scooping up some ground grain mixed with molasses, she walked through the gate of the pen and deposited it in the pig's trough.

"See," she proclaimed as the pig gobbled up the grain, "he's just hungry and he doesn't know any better. Don't be so hard on him. He'll get his come-uppence in the fall when he goes off to hog heaven."

Katie and Ryan knew what happened to the pig in the fall, for they had tasted the delicious Easter ham that Mimi served. However, they weren't entirely convinced it was safe to come down from their perch. Slowly they descended, eyeing the pig cautiously.

They walked over to the cage that held the rest of the small chickens. The children had been very excited when the twelve chicks arrived in the mail two months before, and they had named every one of them. However, the fluffy little chicks had a full suit of feathers now and they had outgrown their cage. They were old enough to be put out into the barnyard to scratch for their own food.

The trouble started when Mimi lifted one chicken from the cage and told her grandson, Ryan, to put it in the pen where the pig was rooting about. She had no idea the pig would react so viciously. The grandchildren were still upset, so Mimi decided to leave the chickens in the cage for another week.

"Let's go and make cookies," she said, trying to get their minds off the barnyard mayhem they had just witnessed.

"That's a good idea." Katie agreed as they all scurried down the hill to the farmhouse. "Can we decorate them?"

\*　　\*　　\*

A week later, a preschool class was scheduled for a tour of the farm. They rode on the hay wagon and picked a pint of strawberries. The last stop on the tour was the animal pen where the children could feed the farm animals. The preschoolers reached out with their tiny hands to feel the horns of the goats and touch the wool of the sheep. Mimi thought it would be interesting for the children to feel the feathers of the young chickens, so she took a chick out of the cage and held it for the children to pet.

As she was showing off the chicken, some other children wanted more feed for the animals. Mimi shifted the chicken into one hand so she could offer the pan of corn to the preschoolers. The chicken unexpectedly fluttered its wings and hopped to the ground. Before Mimi could catch him, he squeezed through the woven-wire fence right in front of the pig!

Quick as a wink, the pig opened his mouth, grabbed the chicken in his jaws and shook his head ferociously. The children and teacher stared in disbelief. Mimi was aghast. Eric, the tractor driver, did a one-handed vault over the fence, snatched the chicken from the pig's mouth and cradled it to his chest as he ran into the barn. It was a daring rescue attempt. Mimi had never seen Eric move so fast.

A few minutes later, Eric emerged from the barn and announced, "The chicken will be all right. He's just a little shaken up."

"Well, that was exciting!" the teacher exclaimed as she exhaled in relief.

"It certainly was a surprise," agreed Mimi.

A week later the chickens had definitely outgrown their cage and had to be released. Mimi put them as far from the animal pen as possible to increase their chances of survival. Every evening Eric scattered a smorgasbord of grain on the ground near the barn. The calf, goats, sheep, chickens, ducks and goose all came to eat. So did the pig that was growing rapidly and was always famished.

Mimi often took kitchen scraps up to the animal pen. As the summer wore on, the number of chickens diminished, and she suspected foul play. She never saw the pig attack any more chickens, but sometimes she found suspicious clumps of feathers and bones on the far side of the pen.

By October, the feisty gray goose and the old rooster were the only birds that came for feeding time. Whenever Mimi threw kitchen scraps over the fence, the pig was the first to come running. He gobbled up everything he could get his mouth on, and gazed after her hungrily as she walked back to the farmhouse.

The pig grew bigger and bigger. From the kitchen window Mimi would sometimes see the huge pig staring down at the farmhouse. She began to wonder if he was merely waiting for kitchen scraps, or if he was eyeing the farmer's plump wife and licking his pork chops.

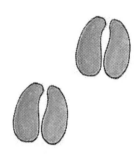

## Pig Facts and Tracks

**Other names:** hog or swine

**Male:** boar or sire    **Female:** sow

**Babies:** piglets    **Group:** herd

**Gestation period:** 114 days

**Favorite food:** corn and other grain, with hay for vitamins. Pigs need minerals, especially salt.

**Life span:** Pigs can live over ten years, but most are sent to market by 7 months

### Interesting fact about pigs:

1. A sow usually gives birth to 8 to 12 piglets, but some litters have been over 20 piglets.

2. A pig is full-grown at 1 ½ to 2 years of age.

3. Hogs have poor eyesight, but a keen sense of smell.

4. Pigs wallow in the mud to keep cool because

they have no sweat glands.

5. Wild hogs come in many sizes from the small pigmy pig that is less than a foot tall, to the giant forest hog that may be over nine feet long. An 11-year old boy in Alabama killed a hog that weighed over 1000 pounds

6. Domesticated pigs can weigh over 500 pounds.

7. Some breeds of pigs have curly tails and some have straight tails.

8. The meat from pigs is called pork, ham and bacon.

9. Besides the meat, we use almost every part of the pig. The hair is used for artist's brushes, insulation and upholstery. The skin and bones are used for glue, clothes, shoes, bone china and footballs. The fat is used for crayons, cosmetics, antifreeze, floor wax, and cement. The glands of pigs are the source for over 40 drugs, including insulin for diabetics.

10. Pig heart-valves are surgically implanted in human hearts to replace diseased valves.

Chapter Nine

# THE GOOSE TWINS

By Kevin and Kyle Larson

# The Goose Twins

## Kevin and Kyle Larson

"What's that?!!"

Farmer Paul was moving hay bales to feed his cows. He used the forklift to bring some bales down from the stack, and saw five white balls roll to the ground.

Getting off his tractor he examined the balls. He discovered they were goose eggs.

"They must belong to those Canadian geese I've seen flying around here," he said to himself.

Three of the eggs were broken as they tumbled down the stack. He picked up the two whole eggs and put them in his truck. After feeding the cows, he headed for home.

"Hi, boys" he greeted his sons." I have something for you. Put these in your incubator."

Eight-year-old Kevin and six-year-old Kyle looked at the eggs with curiosity.

"They sure are a lot bigger than chicken eggs," said Kevin as he laid them in the incubator.

Twenty-two days later, the boys peeked into the incubator and saw two fluffy birds. The twin goslings thought that Kevin and Kyle were their mother and they followed the boys wherever they went. The boys had fun watching the fuzz balls turn into long-necked geese. At first they were cute pets, but by the time they were two months old they were leaving green goose droppings everywhere.

Kyle, influenced by cartoons, named his goose Tweety Bird. Kevin, an honest and keen observer, named his goose Jack Crapper.

One day the boys went to town with their mother. When they returned, they found the goslings swimming happily in their mother's water garden. The twins had eaten the water lilies and other plants and polluted the water with goose dropping. Mother was very sad, but she didn't insist on roast goose for dinner.

The goslings were confined to the fenced tree area. That kept them out of trouble for a while. By the time they were three months old, however, they could fly over the enclosure and they began resting on the front porch. Everyone began to use the side entrance.

One day Kevin and Kyle climbed on their ATV to go to their grandfather's farm that was about a mile away. As they started down the road, Tweety Bird and Jack Crapper flapped their wings and flew about five feet off the ground beside the ATV all the way to the farm.

All summer long the geese flew alongside the ATV whenever the boys went for a ride. Kevin learned that he had to drive fast because geese don't have a slow flying speed. When he tried to slow down, the geese would swoop ahead and land in the middle of the road. Kevin nearly ran over them several times. The neighbors were amused at the sight of two boys and two geese flying down the country road!

As fall approached Kevin and Kyle began to see V-shaped formations of geese flying overhead. Farmer Paul called a family meeting.

"Those geese will die if they stay here all winter. We're not going to keep them in the garage because of their nasty habits. You have to make a choice. Roast goose or take them to the pond where the other geese live and see if they fly south with the flock."

Kevin and Kyle knew they must give up their playmates. They put the geese in a big box and Farmer Paul drove them to the pond. After setting the box on its side so the geese could get out, the family quickly drove away.

The weather turned very cold. Two weeks later when the family returned to the pond, all the geese were gone.

What do you think happened to the geese? Do you think the geese will come back in the spring? Do you think they will remember Kevin and Kyle? You finish writing this story. _____

_____

_____

_____

_____

_____

_____

_____

## Canada Goose Facts and Tracks

**Male**: Gander    **Female**: Goose
(Both are commonly called goose)

**Plural**: Geese

**Babies**: Goslings

**Group**: Flock

**Weight**: 20 to 25 pounds

**Incubation time**:  Eggs hatch in 23-30 days.

**Nest full of eggs**:  Clutch

**Favorite Food**: grass, grain, seeds, berries

**Life span**:  Up to 30 years

**Habits**:  Migrate or fly south in winter.

**Enemies**: raccoons, foxes, owls, snapping turtles

### Interesting Facts:

1.  Mother goose lays one egg a day until she has 5 or 6.  Then she sits on the clutch of eggs and all of the eggs hatch at the same time.

2.  Geese lay eggs in March-May and the gander

stands guard. If an enemy approaches, the gander will hiss, chase after it, and beat it with his wings.

3. Geese mate for life and stay together through all seasons. If one mate dies, the other goose might find a new mate.

4. Goslings can leave the nest in 1 or 2 days and walk, feed and swim.

5. Geese eat for 12 or more hours a day.

6. Geese learn to fly south for the winter so they can find food. This is called migrating.

7. Migrating geese may fly up to 3000 miles and return to the same place in the spring. Geese can fly 1,500 miles or more in 24 hours.

8. They fly in a V-shape and take turns being the leader.

9. In June, geese lose their wing feathers and can't fly (this is called molting). The wing feathers will grow back in 6 weeks.

10. Fifty geese can produce 2 ½ tons of poop in a year.

# Chapter Ten

# THE STORY OF
# SUZY STRAWBERRY

## by Cherie Brooks Reilly

*Picking Strawberries*
*Getting the sweet strawberries*
*From my fingers*
*Down into the basket*
*Without eating all of them*
*Is a problem.*
*The solution is*
*Not solving the problem*
*Until you are full*
*Of answers.*

*Poem by Arnold Adoff*

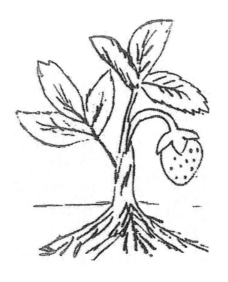

# Suzy Strawberry

by Cherie Brooks Reilly

Once upon a time there was a strawberry plant named Suzy. All winter long she slept under the ground. But when the gentle spring rain began to fall, and the sunshine warmed up the earth, then Suzy woke up. She looked all around at the beautiful world.

Because it was spring, Suzy felt something stirring up in her crown. It wiggled and jiggled and up came some great green leaves, right out of her crown. Soon Suzy felt something else stirring in her crown. And out came a long stem and at the end of the stem appeared some lovely white flowers.

Suzy looked quite pretty in her new spring flowery hat. She looked around and saw that she had some neighbors living close to her. Mrs. Tulip, straight, tall and elegant, had grown up next door to Suzy. Pretty Bluebell grew close to Suzy so they could have a conversation. Little White Flower had sprouted up next to Suzy's roots. And Mr. Sunflower grew very tall and he followed the sun all day long.

One day all the flowers were out in the field talking and visiting and complimenting each other about their pretty flowers. Suddenly, some boys and girls from the nearby school came to the meadow.

When they saw the beautiful flowers, they said, "Oh Teacher, may we pick some and take them back to our school?"

"Yes," said the teacher, "but only pick the ones that I said you could pick."

So they picked Mrs. Tulip, and they picked Pretty Bluebell, and they picked Little White Flower, and they picked Mr. Sunflower, and they took them back to their school.

Now poor Suzy was all alone. She looked around and said, "What's wrong with my flowers? Aren't they as pretty as the rest of the flowers?" She felt very sad. To make matters worse, her pretty white flowers started to fall off. In place of the flowers were some great green globs, right there on top of her head!

"Oh," said Suzy, "I'm so ugly nobody will love me now." And she cried, and cried, and cried.

Well, Suzy was so busy feeling sorry for herself that she didn't notice that those green globs on her head were getting bigger and bigger and bigger, and the sunshine was turning them red.

One day the boys and girls from the nearby school came back to the meadow, and Suzy saw them coming.

"Oh, no," said Suzy. "Those are the boys and girls that didn't like me when I had my pretty white flowers. They're going to hate me now because I'm so ugly. Stay away, boys and girls, I don't want you to see me like this."

But the boys and girls kept coming toward Suzy.

"They think I'm so ugly that they're going to stomp all over me," said Suzy.

The boys and girls came closer and closer to Suzy, and when they were right next to her, they reached down and picked those red things off her head and popped them into their mouths.

Oh, yummy," they said. "These are the most delicious strawberries we've ever tasted. Thank you for making them for us. You are our favorite plant."

Suzy was so happy because she knew that she had done something nice for the boys and girls. She had made them ripe, delicious strawberries.

The End